MIDNIGHT MUNCHIES

MIDNIGHT MUNCHIES

MORE THAN **60** QUICK-FIX SNACKS
By DIANE MORGAN
Photographs by PETER MEDILEK

CHRONICLE BOOKS
SAN FRANCISCO

Library of Congress Cataloging-in-Publication Data available.

ISBN 0-8118-3534-0

Manufactured in China.

Design and illustration by Jennifer Sonderby / Sonderby Design

Photographs by Peter Medilek, Food Look NY

Food styling by Patrik Jaros, Food Look NY

Prop styling by Sonja Jürgens

The photographer wishes to thank the following:
Filipe from Room One, Nancy from Nancy Koltes, Cath from Kar'ikter, Ellen from
Lale, Banu from Terminal NYC.

Special thanks to Eva Turnispeed and Alexx Webber

Distributed in Canada by Raincoast Books
9050 Shaughnessy Street
Vancouver, British Columbia V6P 6E5

10 9 8 7 6 5 4 3 2 1

Chronicle Books LLC
85 Second Street
San Francisco, California 94105

www.chroniclebooks.com

[Page 2: Drew Barrymore's Pop-Tart Special, PAGE 45]

Dedication

To my son, Eric, midnight muncher extraordinaire.

Acknowledgments

After looking at the recipes in this book, you are going to find it hard to believe that I'm a bit of a purist when it comes to food. I shop at farmers' markets as often as I can, buy organic, eat lots of veggies and very little red meat, and pick my fat calories carefully—oh, except for chocolate (there is always room for good chocolate). So, you might ask, what the heck am I doing writing a book called *Midnight Munchies*? My editor and dear friend, Bill LeBlond, had a lot to do with my decision to pursue this project. So did Leslie Jonath, another wonderful Chronicle Books editor. They convinced me to write the book—there are lots of midnight munchers out there—that it would be fun, that I'd come up with great recipes. To the two of you, many thanks, for you were right. This has been an incredibly fun project.

To Amy Treadwell, Michele Fuller, Sarah Bailey, and the others at Chronicle Books who have kept my projects on track and supported my efforts as I travel around the country teaching cooking classes, I am delighted, absolutely delighted, to be working with you. To Sharon Silva, I am thrilled to have you copyediting my book. I've heard you're the best, and you are.

I couldn't have done this book without the help and insatiable appetites of my two teenage children. Eric, the number of times I have been awakened at midnight by the sounds of popcorn popping is uncountable. An empty chips bag and scooped-clean salsa container in the trash can are just two telltale signs of your many late-night kitchen invasions. Molly, ice-cream muncher and smoothie goddess, I know you expect the freezer to be well stocked with frozen fruits, sorbets, and yogurt. When the whim strikes to whip up some drinkable concoction, you always want choices so you can allow your kitchen creativity to flow. This project, you have to agree, kept you abundantly indulged.

Recipe testing and development takes energy, enthusiasm, and diligence. I am deeply grateful to Cheryl Russell for her assistance in the kitchen and multiple runs to the grocery store when we ran out of ingredients.

Many thanks to all the Reed College students, faculty, and staff who stopped by my table, strategically set up in the dining hall, and answered my survey about what favorite foods they eat at midnight. Your insights were brilliant, funny, and helpful.

To my friends who I tempted with calorie-laden munchies and who so generously obliged, many thanks and see you at the gym: Harriet and Peter Watson, Karen Brooks and George Eltman, Margie and Ken Sanders, Marci and Steve Taylor, Priscilla and John Longfield, Georgia and Tad Savinar, Sara Perry, Mary Corpening Barber, Sara Corpening Whiteford, Tori Ritchie, Tonya Holland, Karen Evenden, Josie Jimenez, Summer Jameson, Debbie Adams, Laura Jones, Michele Yurick, Roxanne Murata, Adrienne Silveira, and everyone else at the Pilates studio—Alicia Buoni, Leslie Lewis, Rosanne Bergeron, and Rob Harvey.

To my husband, Greg, whose palate I trust, insights I welcome, and love I cherish.

CONTENTS

2 MOVIE MUNCHIES AND POPCORN MADNESS

3 ROMANTIC MUNCHIES

4 BROKENHEARTED MUNCHIES

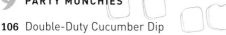

Like Dagwood, no one wants to admit to sneaking into the kitchen late at night to scour the cupboards and survey the refrigerator. But the midnight muncher never goes undiscovered. The empty, crumpled tortilla chips bag stuffed into the garbage and the half-eaten container of salsa left on the counter are clues. The trusty nose of a sleeping pooch always wakes to the scent of popcorn popping. And the bleary-eyed student cramming for a test is heard shuffling down the hall looking for the next caffeine fix.

What is it about those cravings, whims, and munchies that pull us into the kitchen for the quick fix? Anyone can grab a granola bar, sneak a Snickers, or fill a bowl with ice cream. But a true midnight muncher looking for taste and adventure wants more. And that's what this book is all about. *Midnight Munchies* is a collection of fresh twists on the sweet munchies, the salt and crunch cravings, and even the mood munchies for the times when we're blue, blah, or anxious.

I didn't know there were so many muncher types until I surveyed high-school students (my kids' friends), college students, office workers, and *my* "middle-aged" friends. (This last group are the closet munchers, the guilty feelin' ones who refuse to admit to midnight kitchen forays.) With permission from Reed College, I conducted an on-campus survey of over 150 students, faculty, and staff. I strategically set up a table in the dining hall with a big, bold yellow sign, questionnaires, pens, and, of course, the lure of homemade cookies for those who filled out the survey. (I'm no dummy; I know what it takes to get people to stop and answer questions.)

The survey was designed as a series of questions: What do you eat when you are stressed? Feeling blue? Have PMS? I didn't make it gender specific, so most guys just skipped that question. However, being the smart students that they are, some wrote in clever answers, including: "I wouldn't know about PMS, I don't have a uterus." "Yeah, I think my girlfriend deals with that; chocolate, right?" More conventional questions on the survey asked about favorite movie munchies, party munchies, and breakfast-at-midnight munchies. After very unscientifically compiling the answers, I developed the chapters for this book. I saw trends, despite age differences, for what people liked to munch. The chapters reflect those trends.

Realizing that munching crosses all taste desires—sweet, salty, hot and spicy, bitter and sour—I developed recipes that play to these taste-bud sensations. Forget, at least in this book, that extra taste Japanese scientists call *umani,* which translates loosely into "meaty" or "savory." I'm going for big flavors here, not the subtle nuances found in fussy food preparations. You want sweet, you get sweet—go for a big Snickers Bar Shake (page 25). If salty is your midnight craving, then check out the Parmesan, Herb, and Salt–Coated Soft Pretzels (page 32). Puckery Lemon Pudding on Toasted Pound Cake with Fresh Blueberries (page 38) fits the bill for a sour-power late-night treat. Chapter 1 is packed with snacks everyone's taste buds lust after.

Disgustingly large buckets of popcorn and supersize drinks—the items the clumsy guy behind you accidentally spills and are now running like a lava flow right under your seat—might be good enough for the movie theater, but just think of what you can whip up at home. Popcorn surging with zippy spices and hot-pepper sauce, down-home ranch flavors, or a super-cheesy Italian-style mix makes a stay-in movie night an appealing alternative. Every movie munchie in Chapter 2 has the clear advantage of needing only one hand for eating, thereby keeping the remote grease-free.

Mood munchies were a slam-dunk choice for this book. Foods we eat when we're in love, foods we devour when free-falling out of love, the well-documented cravings that ease the PMS time of month, stimulating brain-enriching snacks, big bowls of comfort foods, and anger-relinquishing treats required three full chapters of munchie-filled goodness. Chocolate for love, more chocolate for the broken-hearted, Nutella by the spoonful, soup for the soul, spicy heat to flush the heat of fury. You name the mood, I've got the food.

That wicked time between dusk and dawn, when dinner is over and breakfast hasn't begun, gives the stress junkie plenty of time for consuming and burning calories. Tests and deadlines have their own high-quality munchies associated with them, such as a Red Bull Smoothie (page 73) and Double-the-Buzz Coffee Ice Cream and Espresso Bean Shake (page 77). The sheer youthful energy that keeps college kids (and those of us who still act like them) up until sunrise requires another chapter of munchies all its own. After all, why wait until morning to enjoy breakfast? Mountains of pancakes, crunchy French toast, or eggs and hash browns sizzling on the stove never taste better than at midnight, when dorm lights are burnin' bright.

Midnight Munchies is pegged to the instant-gratification, quick-to-fix crowd—and that crowd also parties. Check out the last chapter on party munchies—plan a party for gals, a party for guys, or party with your beer drinkin' buds. Start the beer flowing and pump up guests' palates with Salt and Savory Golden Almonds (page 111) and Chorizo Macho Nachos (page 113). Have spa-party fun with the Double-Duty Cucumber Dip (page 106), a veggie dip and face mask in one. Strut your cooking skills for an all-out sports-night munchie party. Nothing could be easier than Drunken Shrimp Poached in Beer with Cajun Mayonnaise (page 115). C'mon, football plays are more complicated than the recipe for Texas-in-the-Bag Chili (page 117).

Ultimately, this book is about munchie fulfillment, about hitting the taste buds with big flavors when you want it and how you want it. Who cares the reason—maybe there's none. Midnight is perfect, any time works. Munch freely, munch happily, munch on!

Okay munchers, if you are going to snack at midnight, don't you think having a few snack items on hand would be helpful? Hey, don't let me stop you from making a dash to the supermarket or convenience store, if that's your idea of munchie-binge fun. But it sure is a whole lot easier to reach for a box of popcorn, rip open a bag of chips, or search the freezer for disgustingly rich ice cream when that munch-snack-attack hits.

I realize snacking choices are personal, highly evolved, and even, perhaps, gender specific. However, I think there are some universal favorites that make the top 100 munchie list and, at least for the recipes in this book, ought to be in the fridge, in the freezer, or on the pantry shelf.

IN THE FRIDGE—short, medium, and long shelf life

Short shelf life—to be watched for turning sour, growing mold, and generally getting gross: milk, cream, yogurt, eggs, sour cream, fresh salsa

Medium shelf life—gets moldy and old more slowly: cheese, cream cheese, butter, orange juice, tortillas, fruits and veggies, cookie dough

Long shelf life—fuhgeddaboudit, it will last: Parmesan in the green can, mayonnaise, mustard, ketchup, pickles, olives, maple syrup

IN THE FREEZER—stashing the really good stuff

Bread and cake: bagels, soft pretzels, muffins, pound cake, waffles

Fruits and veggies: individually frozen strawberries, raspberries, blueberries, peaches, peas (oh c'mon, they're good for you)

Ice cream, sorbet, and frozen yogurt (lots of them)

Meaty stuff: chicken nuggets, bacon, sausages

Nuts and seeds: almonds, pecans, cashews, pumpkin seeds, sunflower seeds, sesame seeds (hey, they won't go rancid when kept frozen)

Potatoes: hash browns, Tater Tots

ON THE PANTRY SHELF—ready to grab, won't get stale or moldy

Candy: Heath bars, Snickers bars, Hershey's Kisses, Milk Duds, and so on

Canned foods: black beans, chili with beans, diced jalapeños, chipotle chiles in adobo sauce, coconut milk, chicken broth, canned soup, tuna fish, diced tomatoes

Chocolate: bittersweet and semisweet bars, chips, syrup, fudge topping, Dutch-process cocoa powder, chocolate-covered espresso beans

Crackers (including graham), **cookies** (big fat ones), **chips** (especially tortilla), **Pop-Tarts, and energy bars**

Cereals: your faves, of course, but include rolled oats, Rice Krispies, cornflakes

Drinks: colas, root beer, Red Bull, juices, coffee, teas

Marshmallows: big ones, miniature ones, marshmallow crème

Mixes: muffin, brownie, pancake, macaroni and cheese (cheap and easy)

Nutella and peanut butter (need only a spoon)

Oils: olive oil, vegetable oil, nonstick cooking spray

Pasta, egg noodles, and rice

Popcorn: either micro-magic variety or the old-fashioned kind

Ramen: deserves a category all its own—quick, cheap, no cooking skills required

Spices and extracts: salt, pepper, cayenne, Italian herb seasoning, Cajun seasoning, cinnamon, vanilla

Sauces: barbecue sauce, marinara sauce, hot-pepper sauce

Sugar and sweeteners: granulated sugar, powdered sugar, brown sugar, honey

Never before have I exposed in such graphic detail all the techniques I have learned on my way to becoming a munchie master. But I'll do it here because you have bought my book (or are about to buy my book—please proceed to checkout!) and need to learn the wisdom of my ways. Mastering munchie making requires very few tools and even fewer pieces of equipment. Here is my very short list of essentials. Techniques follow.

If this is all I had in my kitchen, plus, of course, a stove, sink, and refrigerator, I could make everything in this book.

Microwave

Blender

Toaster or toaster oven

2 pots: 1 small, 1 big

2 skillets: 1 small, 1 big

2 rimmed baking sheets

1 set nesting mixing bowls

Measuring cups and spoons

Cutting board

3 sharp knives: 1 paring, 1 chef's, 1 bread

3 openers: 1 bottle, 1 can, 1 wine

Ice cream scoop, stirring spoon, spatula, whisk, and vegetable peeler

Now for the techniques.

MICRO-MAGIC—Or how I use the microwave oven to save time, cleanup, and energy.

Melting: butter, cheese, chocolate, marmalade, peanut butter, marshmallows

Timing is everything and practice makes perfect. Thanks to mom, you've heard that advice before, but this is absolutely true for melting stuff in the microwave. Place whatever food you are going to melt in a microwave-safe bowl, large enough so that if the item bubbles up it won't ooze over the sides and make a mess. Next trick: watch it, watch it, and watch it. It is hard to give precise timing, though I try to in the recipes; however, with practice you'll instinctively get good at it. For instance, I know it takes about 50 seconds to melt a cold stick of butter, whereas 40 seconds is too little and 90 seconds leaves me with butter all over the floor of my microwave. I'd rather err on the side of less time and have to punch in additional seconds than clean up a mess. Chocolate is tricky because it doesn't look like it is melting. Those little squares hold their shape on the outside, but inside they're melted and runny—kinda like chocolate-covered cherries. Definitely err on the side of less time and then stir to melt the rest. When melted in the microwave, chocolate "seizes" if it gets too hot, turning into a grainy, clumpy, unusable mess that tastes burnt—you've been warned.

Warming and softening: milk, cream cheese, ice cream

The beauty of a microwave is its ability to speed up the time it takes for something to soften, as in ice cream or cream cheese. When I want ice cream for a sundae or milk shake, and I don't have a muscle man around to scoop rock-hard ice cream from the container, I just zap it for 10 seconds or a little longer and voilà, I have ice cream ready to scoop. The same works for cream cheese when I want it spreadable immediately. Milk, heated in a mug for hot chocolate, goes from ice cold to perfect sipping temperature in 90 seconds.

Toasting: shelled nuts and seeds (such as sesame)

A little-known technique to the novice cook, toasting nuts in the microwave works perfectly. Spread the nuts on a microwave-safe plate and zap on high until toasty brown. Again, practice and you'll perfect the timing. Use a hot pad to remove the plate, as it gets hot. Let the nuts cool slightly before handling.

Popping Popcorn

Hard-core, popping-popcorn-in-a-skillet purists will consider this blasphemous, but my favorite popcorn-popping mode is in the microwave. Listen, I'm a purist on many levels—for example, margarine is not welcome in my home—this just happens not to be one of them. I like the no-fuss, no-muss approach to popcorn that's ready in 4 minutes.

BLENDER TRICKS— For a smooth operator.

Smoothies, slushies, milk shakes, and frappés work best if you don't overload the blender—tempting as it may be to make just one batch. In addition, if you layer the frozen fruit or ice cream with the liquid stuff, everything will blend more smoothly. Having everything frozen on the bottom tends to clog the blades and overheat the motor. (Ah, she learned from experience. Having burned out— oh, perhaps purposely—an ugly avocado green blender, I now have a beautiful new stainless-steel one.)

TOASTER VERSUS TOASTER OVEN—Go for the multitasker.

Traditional toasters are cheap and straightforward to use. Buy one that can toast bagels and thick slices of bread. However, toaster ovens allow you to caramelize and brown small servings of dessert and gratin dishes, and even bake frozen foods without turning on a big oven. And there is never any problem toasting bagels and other sure-to-get-stuck breads. Convection-style toaster ovens do wonders on reheating pizza. Splurge if you can.

CRUSHING AND CRUMBLING—Who needs a rolling pin when the bottom of a pan will do?

Some munchies require the crushing or crumbling of crackers, candy bars, and cornflakes. Though a rolling pin is a handy tool to own, no one is expecting your kitchen to be that well stocked. So, whether you are feeling in a wham-and-whomp mood or not, the bottom of a pot or small skillet works wonderfully for crushing crunchy foods (as does a hammer). Put the food to be crushed in a heavy, lock-top plastic bag, press or squeeze the bag to get all the air out, seal the bag, lay it on the counter, and pound it with the bottom of the pan until the crunchy stuff is crushed.

A New Twist on Late-Night Munchies

Hey, what do you guys wanna eat? I dunno. Well, tell me. I dunno. Something sweet? Say, an ice cream sandwich? I dunno. Something salty, like chips and dip? I dunno. How 'bout spicy and hot? Or really, really sour? Oh, man, just fix it. You're making me hungry.

[Mac and Cheese on Steroids, PAGE 36]

Cinnamony sweet bread, punctuated with raisins, is warm and toasty straight from the skillet. Oozing with melted cream cheese, this sandwich is a treat any time. Pour a tall glass of milk or make a spot of tea.

2 slices **cinnamon-swirl raisin bread**

2 to 3 tablespoons **cream cheese**, softened

1 tablespoon **butter**, at room temperature

Spread 1 slice of the bread with the cream cheese. Top with the other bread slice. Spread the top of the sandwich with half of the butter.

Heat a skillet over medium heat or preheat a griddle to medium. Place the sandwich, buttered-side down, on the hot surface and grill until nicely browned, 1 to 1½ minutes. While the first side is browning, spread the top of the sandwich with butter. Flip the sandwich and brown the other side, about 1 minute longer. Cut in half and eat while it's hot.

MAKES 1 SANDWICH

There's a whole lotta shakin' going on at midnight when the milk shake munchies hit. Plug in that blender for a double dose of chocolate, caramel, and peanuts.

6 large scoops **Dreyer's Snickers ice cream**

$\frac{1}{2}$ cup **milk**

1 large (3.7 ounces) **Snickers bar**, cut into small pieces

Place half of the ice cream and half of the milk in a blender and scatter half of the candy bar pieces on top. Blend until thick and smooth, although small chunks of candy are desirable. Pour into a tall chilled glass. Repeat with the remaining ingredients to make another milk shake.

SERVES 2

You can bet Jackie Chan doesn't wait around for his ice cream to soften when the midnight snack mood strikes. No way! With lightning speed, his ice cream is out of the freezer and into a hunger-slaying sandwich. Follow his moves—if you can!

1 package (8.6 ounces) **Pepperidge Farm chocolate chunk soft-baked Sausalito cookies**

1 pint **Ben & Jerry's Chocolate Fudge Brownie ice cream**

Remove all 8 cookies from the package and set aside. Remove the lid from the pint of ice cream and set the container upside-down on a cutting board. With a big, sharp knife, and using your best karate "hi-YA" voice, whack down, slicing right through the container to cut it in half. (Don't try this with your bare hand!) Peel the container off each half. Place the halves flat-sides down, and cut each half into 4 thick slices.

Turn 1 cookie bottom-side up, and arrange 2 halves of ice cream (forming a circle) on top. Place another cookie on top, bottom-side down. Repeat to make 4 ice cream sandwiches in all. Eat immediately or wrap in plastic wrap and store in the freezer.

MAKES 4 ICE CREAM SANDWICHES

MUNCHIE TIP
This is my favorite ice cream sandwich combo—chocolate, chocolate, and more chocolate. But the ice cream case is full of possibilities, so play and pick your own favorites.

These balls—crisp and chocolaty with crunchy bits of toffee—have it all over those kid-friendly Rice Krispies treats. Sticky and sweet melted marshmallows and nutty peanut butter glue them together. Believe me, you won't be able to eat just one.

2 cups **Rice Krispies**

$1/4$ cup miniature **semisweet chocolate chips**

2 regular-size (1.4 ounces each) **Heath bars**

$1/2$ cup super chunk **peanut butter**

12 regular-size **marshmallows**

In a large bowl, combine the Rice Krispies and chocolate chips. Leaving the Heath bars in their wrappers, use a heavy object (rolling pin, hammer, back of a metal spoon) to pound and crush the bars into little pieces. Add to the bowl (discard the wrappers!).

Place the peanut butter and marshmallows in a microwave-safe bowl. Cover and microwave on high until hot and gooey, about 1 minute. Working quickly, add to the Rice Krispies mixture. Use a rubber spatula or, better yet, use your hands to mix thoroughly. Form into balls the size of a golf ball. Munch away.

MAKES 16 BALLS

MUNCHIE TIP
No microwave? Place the peanut butter and marshmallows in a heavy saucepan. Stir over low heat until melted.

Take sweet potatoes straight from the can, douse them with a dynamo combo of butter, brown sugar, and candied ginger, and you've got a crusty, caramelized treat. Still hungry? Add a turkey or ham sandwich.

1 can (29 ounces) cut **sweet potatoes** in light syrup

$1/2$ cup firmly packed **golden brown sugar**

2 tablespoons **butter**

2 heaping tablespoons diced **candied ginger**
(See Munchie Tip)

Place an oven rack about 4 inches from the broiler and preheat the broiler.

Drain the sweet potatoes, reserving 2 tablespoons of the syrup. Place the potatoes in a flameproof pie plate. In a microwave-safe bowl or in a small saucepan, combine the reserved syrup, the sugar, butter, and candied ginger and microwave on high until the butter melts, about 45 seconds.

Stir until the sugar is melted. Spoon this mixture over the sweet potatoes. Broil until bubbly hot and crusty, about 5 minutes. Eat them while they're hot.

MAKES 2 NORMAL-SIZE SERVINGS OR 1 PIG-OUT-SIZE SERVING

MUNCHIE TIP
Sliced candied ginger, also known as crystallized ginger, comes in a box and is found in the Asian foods section or the baking section of most supermarkets.

Say good-bye to the ho-hum fluffer-nutter sandwich and try this souped-up version. Peanut butter and marshmallow crème may be good enough for some folks, but for this ultimo sandwich, check out the addition of banana slices and drizzles of chocolate syrup. With a nod toward healthy eating, I like my 'wich best on toasted whole-wheat bread!

2 slices of your favorite **sandwich bread**

A glob of **peanut butter**

A big, fat spoonful of **marshmallow crème**

$1/2$ **banana**, thinly sliced

Chocolate syrup in a squeeze bottle

Toast the bread. Smear the peanut butter on 1 slice. Spread the marshmallow crème on the other slice. Arrange the banana slices in a single layer on top of the peanut butter. Squeeze the bottle of chocolate syrup, drizzling as much chocolate over the bananas as you like. Place the marshmallow-coated slice, marshmallow-side down, on top. Cut the sandwich in half, or eat it whole.

MAKES 1 SANDWICH

No, it's not fireworks in the oven, just the exciting sounds of seeds popping and crackling as they roast. These are perfect for late-night snacking, great with beer at a party, and couldn't be better pulled from a backpack when afternoon hunger pangs hit.

2 tablespoons **olive oil**

1½ teaspoons **coarse sea salt** or **kosher salt**

¼ teaspoon **cayenne pepper**

2 teaspoons ground **cumin**

1 cup raw **pumpkin seeds**

1 cup raw **sunflower seeds**

Preheat the oven to 400°F. In a large bowl, combine the oil, salt, cayenne, and cumin. Toss in the pumpkin and sunflower seeds and stir until thoroughly coated.

Spread out the seeds on a rimmed baking sheet. Roast until fragrant and nicely browned, about 10 minutes. Start munching as soon as they're cool enough to eat.

MAKES 2 CUPS

Hanging out with friends? Stirring a pitcher of martinis or pouring some special single-malt scotch? These are the munchies of choice: crunchy, peppery-hot almonds peek out of oversize olives—just the right size for one big bite.

1 tablespoon **olive oil**

1 teaspoon **coarse sea salt** or **kosher salt**

$\frac{1}{2}$ teaspoon **cayenne pepper**

1 cup raw, skin-on whole **almonds**

1 jar (7 ounces) queen-size **olives stuffed with pimientos**

$\frac{1}{3}$ cup **gin**

Preheat the oven to 350°F. In a bowl, combine the oil, salt, and cayenne. Toss in the nuts and stir until thoroughly coated. Spread out the nuts on a rimmed baking sheet and roast until fragrant and nicely browned, 12 to 14 minutes. Cool the nuts, stirring once while they cool.

While the nuts are roasting, rinse the olives quickly under water and pat dry with paper towels. Put in a bowl with the gin and stir to mix. Let marinate while the nuts are cooling.

When the nuts are cool, drain the gin, but don't throw it out—drink it or save it. Without removing the pimientos, stuff a nut into each olive.

MAKES 1 CUP NUTS, MORE THAN ENOUGH TO STUFF A JAR OF OLIVES

Warm pretzels from a street vendor or out of a hot box at the ballpark are yummy, but these are better—much better. Spiced up with hot-pepper sauce, crusted with Parmesan, and flavored with herbs and salt, two of these may not be enough. Not to worry, they come six to a box.

2 frozen **soft pretzels**

⅛ teaspoon **hot-pepper sauce** such as Tabasco

¼ teaspoon **water**

1½ tablespoons grated **Parmesan cheese**

1 teaspoon **Italian herb seasoning**

⅓ packet **coarse pretzel salt** (from soft pretzel box)

Preheat the oven to 400°F. Place the pretzels on a rimmed baking sheet. In a little bowl, mix together the hot-pepper sauce and water. Use your finger to coat the top side of the pretzels with this mixture. Sprinkle on the cheese, herbs, and salt. Bake until crusty and golden brown, about 5 minutes. Eat 'em while they're hot.

SERVES 1

MUNCHIE TIP
These are perfect for a party. Double, triple, quadruple the recipe—you get the idea—as they're easy to make and fun. For an extra treat, serve them with dipping sauces, such as warm marinara sauce, grainy mustard, or pesto thinned with olive oil.

There's no messin' with Texas when it comes to dips and chips. Pop open a can of snappy hot tomatoes and green chiles, melt down a hunk of Velveeta, and you've got yourself a cheese-spiked dip worthy of a late-night party—hot, gooey, and finger-lickin' good.

3/4 pound **Velveeta cheese**, cut into 1-inch cubes

1 can (10 ounces) **RO*TEL diced tomatoes and green chiles**, well drained

Juice of 1/2 **lime**

1 bag (20 ounces) **tortilla chips**

Place the cheese in a large, microwave-safe bowl. Microwave on high, stirring once or twice, until melted, about 2 1/2 minutes. Stir in the tomatoes and chiles, blending thoroughly. Microwave until hot, about 1 minute longer. Stir in the lime juice. Serve hot accompanied with a big bowl of chips.

MAKES ABOUT 2 CUPS DIP

MUNCHIE TIP
Of course, this dip is primo with chips, but try it drizzled over Tater Tots, chicken nuggets, or soft pretzels.

Warm curry paste in a pot, throw in some coconut milk, crunch up some ramen noodles, and you're five minutes away from a Thai curry noodle soup. Have leftover chicken or veggies? Chop and toss in. Slivers of green onion or chopped cilantro leaves will add color and great flavor to the soup.

1 tablespoon **vegetable oil**

1/2 teaspoon **red curry paste** (see Munchie Tip)

1 teaspoon **yellow curry paste** (see Munchie Tip)

1 can (13.5 ounces) **unsweetened coconut milk**

2 cups **water**

2 packages (3 ounces each) **instant ramen noodle soup**, roast chicken flavor

1 tablespoon fresh **lime juice**

Place a medium saucepan over medium-low heat and add the oil and curry pastes. Stir to combine and cook until fragrant, less than a minute. Add half of the coconut milk and stir until smooth. Increase the heat to medium-high. Add the rest of the coconut milk and the water and bring to a simmer. Before opening the packages of ramen, crunch the noodles, breaking them into small pieces. Add the contents of 1 flavoring pack to the soup and stir to blend. Discard or save the other pack for another use. Add the noodles and cook until tender, about 2 minutes, then stir in the lime juice. Now is when you would toss in any chicken or veggies and top with green onions or cilantro. Serve immediately.

MAKES 2 HUGE OR 3 REGULAR SERVINGS

MUNCHIE TIP
Red, yellow, and even green curry paste is available in small jars and cans at supermarkets or Asian food stores. Red curry paste is made of ground red chiles, herbs, and spices and packs a punch. Use more (or less) to please your taste buds. Keeps forever in the fridge.

Unadulterated mac and cheese in the blue box is okay for kids, but serious munchers are looking for big flavor and crunch. Chunks of salsa, as mild or hot as you like, mingle with the cheese-coated macaroni, and all is covered with crushed Triscuits and more cheese. Zap this under the broiler for a heaping bowl of bubbly, crisp-crunchy delight.

1 box (7.25 ounces) **macaroni and cheese**

½ cup **salsa** (see Munchie Tip)

About 40 **Triscuits**

1 cup (4 ounces) shredded **sharp Cheddar cheese**

Prepare the macaroni and cheese according to package directions. Stir in the salsa. Spoon into a flameproof 1½-quart baking dish.

MUNCHIE TIP
Any kind of salsa will work: tomato, roasted tomato, pico de gallo, tomatillo. Use your favorite.

Preheat the broiler. While the broiler is preheating, place the crackers in a lock-top plastic bag, squeeze out all the air, and seal the bag. Use a rolling pin or the bottom of a heavy pot to thwack and pound the crackers until finely crushed. You should have about 1 heaping cup. Place the crushed crackers in a bowl and mix in the cheese. Scatter this mixture evenly over the macaroni.

Place under the broiler and broil until bubbly and golden brown, about 3 minutes. Spoon into bowls and serve immediately.

MAKES 1 HUMUNGO, 2 BIG, OR 4 REGULAR SERVINGS

Perk up your taste buds with these salty, fiery-spiced nuts. Pull out some cheese (even string cheese will do), pop open a beer or can of soda, and check the stats on ESPN.

3 tablespoons **butter**

1 tablespoon **hot-pepper sauce** such as Tabasco

2 teaspoons **sugar**

1½ teaspoons **coarse sea salt** or **kosher salt**

2 cups (about ½ pound) **pecan halves**

Preheat the oven to 400°F. Place the butter in a large microwave-safe bowl and microwave on high until melted, about 40 seconds. Alternatively, place in a medium saucepan and melt on top of the stove. Stir in the hot-pepper sauce, sugar, and salt. Toss in the pecans and stir until thoroughly coated.

Spread out the nuts on a rimmed baking sheet and roast until fragrant and nicely browned, about 10 minutes. They'll crisp as they cool.

MAKES 2 CUPS

MUNCHIE TIP
Feeding a crowd? Double the recipe. If you want the munchies to last (are you kidding?), then freeze these and reheat at 400°F for just a couple of minutes before serving.

PUCKERY LEMON PUDDING ON TOASTED POUND CAKE WITH FRESH BLUEBERRIES

Summer snackin' never tasted so good. A big dollop of extra-lemony pudding flows over the ⁄ sugar-crusted edges of toasted pound cake. Fresh-from-the-market blueberries burst forth with every bite. Yummm.

1 (10.75 ounces) frozen **all-butter pound cake**

1 package (3.4 ounces) **lemon flavor Jell-O instant pudding**

1³/₄ cups ice-cold **milk**

3 tablespoons fresh **lemon juice**

1 pint **blueberries**

Remove the pound cake from the freezer and allow to thaw partially while you make the pudding. In a medium bowl, whisk the pudding mix with the milk until thickened, about 2 minutes. Stir in the lemon juice and beat until smooth. Set aside.

Cut the pound cake into 6 or 8 thick slices. Toast, or broil on both sides, until golden brown. Place a slice of toasted pound cake on a plate. Spoon on a big dollop of pudding, and scatter the blueberries on top. Eat immediately.

SERVES 6 to 8

MUNCHIE TIP
You really don't need 5 or 7 friends or family members to enjoy this dessert. Cut as many slices of pound cake as you want and stick the rest back in the freezer. Mound on as much pudding as you like and refrigerate the rest for later. (Did I mention how great this is for breakfast?)

This midnight rummage through the condiment shelves of the refrigerator is deli-delicious and easy to fix. Want something even faster than a hard-boiled egg? Fry one—over easy. Slip it right out of the pan and onto the sandwich. Be warned: Oozy-warm egg yolk will be running down your fingers. Grab a napkin.

1 tablespoon or more **mayonnaise**

2 slices **Russian rye bread**, lightly toasted

2 teaspoons or more **Dijon mustard**

1 hard-boiled **egg** (See Munchie Tip)

1 kosher baby **dill pickle**, cut lengthwise into thin slices

2 or 3 thin slices **sweet onion** such as Vidalia, Maui, or Walla Walla

Slather the mayonnaise on 1 slice of toast. Spread the mustard on top. Wipe any remaining mayo and mustard from the spreading knife on the other slice of toast. Using an egg slicer or sharp paring knife, thinly slice the egg crosswise. Arrange overlapping slices of egg on the mustard-coated bread slice. Place pickle slices over the egg, and then add the onion. Top with the other slice of bread, mayo-wiped-slice down. Slice in half and munch away.

MAKES 1 SANDWICH

MUNCHIE TIP
To hard boil an egg properly so that no yucky green color coats the yolk, proceed as follows: Place the eggs in a small saucepan. Add cold water to cover by 1 inch and throw in a pinch of salt. Bring to a boil, and then immediately reduce the temperature to low; the water should barely simmer. Set a timer for 11 minutes. As soon as the timer goes off, pour off the boiling water and run cold water over the eggs until they are cool enough to handle. Peel under running water. If you're not using the eggs immediately, leave the shells on and refrigerate for up to 5 days. Write "HB" on the eggshells with a pencil to indicate they've been cooked.

If you can't pucker up with someone you love, then pucker up with a full-throttle dose of vitamin C. Big, fat slices of an orange are topped with melted marmalade for a double-whammy, healthful treat. Indeed, there is citrus sunshine at midnight.

1 navel **orange**

¼ cup **orange marmalade**

Cinnamon graham crackers

Peel the orange and remove the white pith. Cut crosswise into thick slices, and arrange the slices on a plate. Put the marmalade in a microwave-safe bowl and melt on high until bubbly hot, about 1 minute (or use a small saucepan on the stove top). Spoon over the sliced orange and eat immediately. Munch cinnamon grahams on the side, they add the perfect crunch.

SERVES 1

2

Movie Munchies and Popcorn Madness

The beauty of movie food, as Edwin Shoemaker (inventor of the La-Z-Boy recliner) would tell you, is the ability to eat it with one hand. The other hand is for holding the remote control. All the usual movie candy qualifies— Junior Mints, Sour Patch Kids, Swizzlers, Raisinets—but popcorn tops the list. Chair back, popcorn in lap, hit the "play" button— movie time!

[Mexicali Rose Popcorn, PAGE 44]

"Mexicali Rose, stop crying . . . every night you'll know that I'll be pining" for some of that buttery-spicy-hot popcorn of yours.

4 tablespoons (½ stick) **butter**

½ package (0.5 ounce) **Lawry's taco spices and seasonings**

1 teaspoon **hot-pepper sauce** such as Tabasco

1 bag (3 ounces) almost-fat-free, butter-flavored **microwave popcorn**

Place the butter, taco spices, and hot-pepper sauce in a small, microwave-safe bowl. Microwave on high until bubbly hot, about 1½ minutes. Set aside.

Pop the popcorn according to the package directions. Immediately open the bag and pour the popcorn into a large bowl. Toss with the melted butter mixture. Serve at once.

MAKES ABOUT 12 CUPS

Have you ever wanted to know movie stars' fun food favorites? If you ask Drew Barrymore what she likes to munch on, she'll tell you she loves Pop-Tarts. But does she add smear or not? Check out these strawberry Pop-Tarts. Hot from the toaster, smear 'em with this dreamy, creamy, strawberry-cheesecake-tasting spread.

4 ounces strawberry-flavored **cream cheese**, softened (see Munchie Tip)

4 tablespoons **sour cream**

1 1/2 tablespoons **powdered sugar**

1 teaspoon **vanilla extract**

Pinch of **salt**

1 box strawberry **Pop-Tarts**

In a medium bowl, beat together the cream cheese and 2 tablespoons of the sour cream until completely smooth. Add the rest of the sour cream and mix thoroughly. Add the powdered sugar, vanilla, and salt and mix until smooth.

Toast as many Pop-Tarts as you like. Use a knife to smear the top of each Pop-Tart with the cream cheese spread. Eat them while they're hot. Refrigerate any remaining cream cheese for another night.

MAKES ABOUT 1 CUP STRAWBERRY SMEAR

MUNCHIE TIP
Softening a container of cream cheese quickly is a snap. Pop it in the microwave and warm it for about 20 seconds or so.

The King, the Hunk, loved his snacks—junk food galore. The peanut butter, mayo, and banana sandwich was one, but melt-in-your-mouth caramel was another. Sway your hips, belt out a few bars of "Heartbreak Hotel," and blend this decadent shake.

½ pint **Häagen-Dazs dulce de leche ice cream**

½ **banana**, sliced

¼ cup **milk**

10 **Milk Duds**, cut in half

2 tablespoons miniature **semisweet chocolate chips**

Chocolate shavings for garnish

Combine all the ingredients, except chocolate shavings, in a blender. Blend until thick and smooth. Top with the shavings and enjoy.

MAKES 1 BIG SHAKE

If watching a foreign flick makes you hunger for Mediterranean food, try this buttery, herby, cheesy popcorn combo. Maybe it's not as exciting as *osso buco Milanese* (nor as fun to pronounce), but it sure is easier to make.

4 tablespoons (½ stick) **butter**

2 tablespoons finely chopped fresh **rosemary** (See Munchie Tip)

1 bag (3 ounces) almost-fat-free, butter-flavored **microwave popcorn**

⅓ cup grated **Parmesan cheese**

Salt

Place the butter and rosemary in a small, microwave-safe bowl. Microwave on high until bubbly hot, about 1½ minutes. Set aside.

Pop the popcorn according to the package directions. Immediately open the bag and pour the popcorn into a large bowl. Toss with the melted rosemary butter, and then the Parmesan. Add salt to taste. Serve at once.

MAKES ABOUT 12 CUPS

MUNCHIE TIP
No fragrant fresh rosemary in the house or garden? Use Italian herb seasoning as an easy, off-the-shelf alternative.

Lusting for an Italian man in your life, with dark seductive eyes, thick black hair, and a sly smile? When the words "you are enchanting" cross his lips, melt, melt completely, like the butter in this popcorn.

4 tablespoons (½ stick) **butter**

1 package (0.6 ounce) **Good Seasons Zesty Italian salad dressing mix**

1 bag (3 ounces) almost-fat-free, butter-flavored **microwave popcorn**

Salt

Place the butter and salad dressing mix in a small, microwave-safe bowl. Microwave on high until bubbly hot, about 1½ minutes. Set aside.

Pop the popcorn according to the package directions. Immediately open the bag and pour the popcorn into a large bowl. Toss with the melted butter mixture. Add salt to taste. Serve at once.

MAKES ABOUT 12 CUPS

Herd your friends together and head 'em on out to the video store to rent a nightful of Westerns. Pick the best: Gary Cooper in *High Noon*, John Wayne in *Red River*, and Mel Brooks's *Blazing Saddles*. Pop up a couple of rounds of popcorn and settle in for a spell, pardners.

4 tablespoons (½ stick) **butter**

1 package (0.4 ounce) **Hidden Valley Ranch salad dressing mix**

1 bag (3 ounces) almost-fat-free, butter-flavored **microwave popcorn**

Salt

Place the butter and salad dressing mix in a small, microwave-safe bowl. Microwave on high until bubbly hot, about 1½ minutes. Set aside.

Pop the popcorn according to the package directions. Immediately open the bag and pour the popcorn into a large bowl. Toss with the melted butter mixture. Add salt to taste. Serve at once.

MAKES ABOUT 12 CUPS

Movie party time! Invite friends, rent some movies, and have a serve-yourself sundae bar. Pick a theme, from all-time classics—*Citizen Kane, Casablanca, On the Waterfront*—or musicals—*Singin' in the Rain, The Wizard of Oz*—to comedies—*Some Like It Hot, Annie Hall, Soapdish*—or shoot 'em ups—*Butch Cassidy and the Sundance Kid, The Godfather, Pulp Fiction*. Keep containers of ice cream on ice, toppings warm, and have mega bowls of movie candy on hand for sprinkling on top. All you need are spoons, bowls, and napkins and a big sofa and lots of pillows.

Multiple quarts or half gallons of your favorite **ice cream** such as fudge brownie, mint chocolate chip, strawberries and cream, vanilla, Milky Way bar, rocky road

Several jars of **toppings** such as fudge sauce, pineapple topping, caramel, marshmallow crème

Candy garnishes such as Mini M&M's, chopped up Bon Bons, Raisinets, Gummy Bears, Milk Duds, chopped Nestlé Crunch bars, chopped Twix bars

To set up the buffet, fill a big, wide bowl or large rectangular pan with ice. Take the tops off the ice cream containers and nestle the containers in the ice. Have ice cream scoops ready.

Warm the various toppings and arrange on a tray with serving spoons.

Place the candy garnishes in individual bowls and have a serving spoon in each. Set out bowls, spoons, and napkins for everyone. Eat and enjoy.

SERVES 6 TO 12, DEPENDING ON HOW MUCH YOU BUY

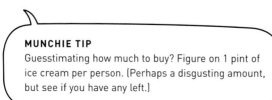

MUNCHIE TIP
Guesstimating how much to buy? Figure on 1 pint of ice cream per person. (Perhaps a disgusting amount, but see if you have any left.)

Romantic Munchies

A perfect date, an invitation to come up, a midnight snack…Linger in the kitchen, lounge on the sofa, nibble slowly, longingly, loving every bite. Seductively rich chocolate? French champagne? Sugar-dusted grapes? Red wine and cheese? What shall it be with thee?

Chocolate lovers unite, dipping blissfully and romantically into a shared bowl of decadent delight. Here, thick, rich, bittersweet chocolate with a hint of cinnamon and a subtle spark of spice enrobes berries and bananas. Perfect for body painting, too!

1 bar (4 ounces) best-you-can-buy **bittersweet chocolate**, broken into small pieces

¼ cup **heavy** (whipping) **cream**

¼ teaspoon ground **cinnamon**

Pinch of freshly ground **black pepper**

1 pint big, ripe **strawberries**, with stems intact

1 **banana**, cut into 1-inch chunks

Place the chocolate, cream, cinnamon, and pepper in a small, microwave-safe bowl. (Trust me here about adding the pepper—it's fabulous.) Microwave on high until the chocolate is melted, about 1 minute. Alternatively, place the ingredients in the top of a double boiler and warm over barely simmering water until melted, 3 to 5 minutes. Stir until smooth.

Pour the chocolate into a serving bowl. Arrange the fruit on a plate. Dip and indulge.

SERVES 2

A night to celebrate—a bottle of bubbly; sugar-coated crisp grapes at the bottom of the flutes; runny, yummy Brie on toast thins; and a knockout date. Make it last.

1 bunch **seedless grapes**, preferably Red Flame

1/2 cup **sugar**

1/2 **baguette**, thinly sliced

1 wedge (about 1/4 pound) **Brie cheese**, at room temperature

1 1/2 teaspoons freshly cracked **black pepper**

1 bottle (750 ml) **champagne**, chilled

Remove the grapes from the stems, rinse under cold water, and shake off the excess water. Place the sugar in a medium bowl. Roll the grapes in the sugar until well coated. Arrange in a single layer on a plate or baking sheet and freeze. They should be frozen within an hour or so.

Preheat the broiler. Arrange the bread slices in a single layer on a baking sheet and broil until lightly toasted. Turn the bread slices over and toast the other side. Set aside to cool.

Place the Brie on a microwave-safe serving plate. Microwave on high until the cheese begins to get runny, about 30 seconds. Sprinkle the pepper over the top.

Set out the warm cheese with the toasted bread. Uncork the champagne. Remove the grapes from the freezer. Place several grapes in the bottom of each champagne flute and serve the rest in a bowl. Celebrate!

SERVES 2 OR MORE

Picture it: One bowl of steaming-hot pasta, two forks, and you and your date slurping up noodles coated with an herb-infused sauce—noses almost touching, forks twirling, and lips close. Giggle and have fun.

1/2 pound dried **spaghetti**

1 tablespoon **olive oil**

1 clove **garlic**, minced

1 1/2 cups prepared **marinara pasta sauce** (See Munchie Tip)

1/4 cup chopped fresh **basil**

1/4 cup chopped fresh **parsley**

Cook the spaghetti in a large pot of salted boiling water until tender but with a bite—al dente—about 10 minutes or so.

While the pasta is cooking, heat the oil in a small saucepan over medium-low heat. Add the garlic and cook until soft and fragrant, but not browned, about 1 minute. Add the marinara sauce and bring to a simmer. Cook for 5 minutes and then stir in the herbs. Simmer for 2 minutes longer to blend the flavors.

Drain the pasta, but don't rinse it. Rinsing takes away that lovely starchy quality of pasta. Immediately pour it into a warmed bowl. Spoon the pasta sauce over the top. Hand a fork to your mate, take a fork for yourself, each lean over the bowl, and slurp away.

SERVES 2

MUNCHIE TIP
Doctoring up canned or bottled pasta sauces, even the best of them, with garlic and fresh herbs takes a ho-hum sauce from edible to delicious. Add as much or as little as you like.

Imagine a romantic night in Venice: starry sky, full moon, arm in arm in a gondola, serenaded, as you slowly drift down the Grand Canal. Re-create a bit of the romance by serving your love Venice's most famous drink, the Bellini, perfect for a balmy summer evening as the sun goes down, just the two of you on the terrace. The romance of Venice won't be far away.

2 very ripe **peaches**, preferably white

1 bottle (750 ml) **Prosecco** (Italian sparkling wine), chilled

Peel and pit the peaches. Purée the flesh in a blender or food processor until perfectly smooth. Pour about 1 inch or more of the peach purée in the bottom of 2 champagne flutes. Top off with the Prosecco. Stir gently, just once, to blend. Take a sip, smell the magic fragrance of peaches, toast your love, and sip some more.

SERVES 2 (WITH SEVERAL REFILLS!)

Anticipating *le hot date* and that suggestive question, "Do you want to come up?" Continue the night in style by uncorking a soft, rich, and velvety Merlot. Offer a truffle and watch as the blissful taste of deeply rich, bittersweet chocolate crosses your date's lips and melts into ecstasy. Lovers' whispers come next . . .

4 ounces **bittersweet chocolate**, very finely chopped

½ cup **heavy** (whipping) **cream**

1 tablespoon **Grand Marnier** or other orange-flavored liqueur

3 tablespoons Dutch-process **cocoa powder**

½ teaspoon ground **cinnamon**

Place the chocolate in a heatproof medium bowl. Bring the cream just to a boil in a small saucepan on the stove top, or place in a microwave-safe bowl and microwave on high until it just begins to boil, about 1 minute. Pour over the chocolate, wait 2 minutes, and then stir gently until smooth. Stir in the liqueur. Cover and refrigerate until firm, about 40 minutes.

Line a baking sheet with parchment paper. Using a teaspoon, scoop up small portions of the chocolate and arrange them on the baking sheet. You should have 20 in all. Roll each portion between your palms into a ball. Don't form perfect balls; truffles look *très* French when they are a bit irregular in shape.

In a small bowl, mix together the cocoa and cinnamon. Roll each truffle in the cocoa mixture. Cover and refrigerate for up to 1 week, or freeze until ready to use. Remove from the refrigerator 10 to 20 minutes before serving. If frozen, thaw 30 minutes before serving.

MAKES 20 TRUFFLES

A bit of midnight kitchen fun turns these basic sugar cookies into melt-in-the-mouth snickerdoodles when rolled in cinnamon-flavored cocoa. Smack in the middle is a divinely rich, warm kiss of chocolate. Got milk?

1½ tablespoons Dutch-process **cocoa powder**

1 teaspoon ground **cinnamon**

1 package (18 ounces) **Break 'n Bake sugar cookies**

20 **Hershey's Kisses**, unwrapped

Preheat the oven to 350°F. Have ready 2 rimmed baking sheets. In a small bowl, mix together the cocoa powder and cinnamon.

Break apart the cookies and roll each piece into a ball. Roll the balls in the cocoa mixture and place 2 inches apart on the ungreased baking sheets. Bake the cookies for 11 minutes and then remove from the oven. Place a chocolate kiss in the center of each cookie, pressing down slightly. Return the cookies to the oven and bake until nicely browned, 2 to 3 minutes longer. Cool briefly; eat while they're warm.

MAKES 20 COOKIES

MUNCHIE TIP
No need to make all 20 cookies. (Are you kidding?) Seal up the package, keep refrigerated, and make another batch later.

BROKENHEARTED MUNCHIES

Unfortunately, fixing feelings with food is mainly a girl thing. Fortunately, there are some pretty darn good things to eat! Full-throttle anger requires a cool-down treat. Nutella mellows the moodiness after *le bad date*. Drowning our sorrows with a bowlful of soup brings comfort. And that bumpy road with the beau has its own metaphoric treat. Cook—eat—get over the loser.

[Rocky Roach Chocolate Fudge Sundae, PAGE 64]

Feed your soul when a relationship goes sour. Food as therapy works best when you relate the food to the mood. Rocky relationship, rocky road ice cream—makes perfect sense.

2 large scoops **rocky road ice cream**

A big, fat spoonful of **marshmallow crème**

2 tablespoons chopped **pecans**, toasted (see Munchie Tip)

Hot fudge sauce

Scoop the ice cream into a bowl—looks like it better be a big one. Spoon the marshmallow crème over the top. Sprinkle on the toasted nuts, and drizzle on lots of fudge sauce.

MAKES 1 DECADENT, BUT DESERVING, SERVING

MUNCHIE TIP
Use a little 'wave magic to toast nuts. Place the nuts on a microwave-safe plate. Microwave on high for 2 minutes. Stir the nuts and microwave until toasty brown, 2 to 3 minutes longer. Keep an eye on the nuts; they can go from crisp to burnt in no time. And use a hot pad to avoid burns.

Creamy-dreamy, tongue-pleasing Nutella, straight from the jar with a spoon, can salve most emotional wounds, but just a moment in the kitchen turns out a plateful of ecstasy. Take fork in hand, plop on the couch, and flood your mouth with delight. *Now,* take all the time you need to feel sorry for yourself.

1 thick slice **challah** or other rich egg bread

2 to 3 tablespoons **Nutella**

2 tablespoons **orange marmalade**, at room temperature

Toast the bread until golden brown and place on a plate. In a small saucepan, warm the Nutella on the stove top over low heat, or warm in a microwave-safe cup in the microwave on high for about 20 seconds. Gently drizzle or spread the Nutella on the toast, and then spoon the marmalade over the top. Eat immediately.

SERVES 1

MUNCHIE TIP
This love-lost remedy works equally well with toasted pound cake.

When your love life has soured, gather together, girlfriends, and replay your Girl Scout days. Forget the open flame and one-match-fire badge (which you probably never got), and scoot these s'mores under the broiler for a wickedly delicious treat. Note the grown-up addition of fine chocolate, coconut, and Craisins. After all, you deserve the best.

1 bar (4 ounces) high-quality **bittersweet chocolate** (see Munchie Tip)

8 chocolate **graham crackers** or **Chocolate Chip Cookies**

⅓ cup sweetened **shredded coconut**

1 bag (6 ounces) **Ocean Spray Craisins** (sweetened dried cranberries)

12 **Kraft Jet-Puffed marshmallows**

Preheat the broiler. Break the chocolate bar into ½-ounce sections. Place 1 chocolate section on each of 4 of the graham crackers. Place on a microwave-safe plate and microwave on high until the chocolate begins to melt, about 1½ minutes. Spread the softened chocolate to cover each cracker. Sprinkle a heaping tablespoon of coconut on top of the chocolate. Scatter Craisins over the coconut, using as many as you like. Tear the marshmallows in half and arrange 6 halves on top of each cracker.

Place the loaded graham crackers on a baking sheet. Broil until the marshmallows are toasty brown and melted, about 45 seconds. Don't burn 'em, girls. Place a graham cracker on top of the marshmallows to make a sandwich, smoosh them down, giggle, and enjoy.

MAKES 4 S'MORES

MUNCHIE TIP
Elevating s'mores to the divine requires fabulous, rich, dark chocolate. Go for the good stuff that you find in the baking aisle, not the candy aisle, of supermarkets.

My friend had a bad date and was feeling sorry for herself and wanted something to eat. She called me, and all I could think of for complete comfort was my mom's tuna noodle casserole. But she didn't want to cook noodles because she didn't want to wash a pot. So, here's my solution. Hey, go the extra mile and toss in some frozen peas (they're good for you) and add a yummy-crusty broiled top of Parmesan and bread crumbs—it takes only a minute to throw the whole thing together.

1 can (10¾ ounces) condensed **cream of mushroom soup**

1 can (6 ounces) **tuna fish**, drained

½ teaspoon **Worcestershire sauce** (optional)

2 packages (3 ounces each) instant **ramen noodle soup**, roast chicken flavor

½ cup frozen **peas** (optional)

¼ cup plain **bread crumbs**

¼ cup grated **Parmesan cheese**

Combine the contents of the can of mushroom soup with 1 can of hot water in a 1½-quart microwave-proof, flameproof bowl. Use a fork to flake the tuna and stir in. Mix in the Worcestershire sauce, if using. Before opening the packages of ramen, crunch the noodles, breaking them into small pieces. Discard both the flavor packs, or save for another use. Stir the noodles into the soup mixture. Stir in the peas, if using. Cover and microwave on high for 7 minutes.

Meanwhile, preheat the broiler. Mix together the bread crumbs and Parmesan. Remove the cover from the casserole, stir once more, and then sprinkle the bread crumb mixture over the top. Broil until toasty brown, about 2 minutes. Grab a spoon and dig in.

MAKES 2 NORMAL-SIZE SERVINGS OR 1 FEELING-SORRY-FOR-YOUR-SELF SERVING WITH PLENTY FOR LEFTOVERS

With love gone wrong, you need more than an ordinary root beer float to pick up the spirits. Get chillin' with frozen root beer, add a hefty mound of chunky caramel ice cream, and whirl into a better mood. Take a bubble bath while you're waiting for the root beer to freeze.

2 bottles draft-style **root beer** such as Henry Weinhard or Thomas Kemper, chilled

½ pint **Ben & Jerry's Triple Caramel Chunk ice cream**

Pour 1 bottle of the root beer into an 8-inch square pan (or a pan close to that size). Stir with a spoon to defizz some of the carbonation. Place the pan in the freezer and chill until mostly frozen, about 2 hours. This is a perfectly good time to smolder over love lost.

Use a fork to break the frozen root beer into chunks. Place the chunks in a blender. Spoon in the ice cream, and then add about half of the remaining bottle of root beer. Blend until thick and smooth. Pour into a chilled tall glass. Add extra root beer, if desired. Taste the creaminess, love the fizz, and forget the guy.

MAKES 1 BIG FRAPPÉ

STRESSIN' FOR A TEST OR DEADLINE MUNCHIES

Geez, that rewrite of *The Great Gatsby* paper due tomorrow looked a whole lot better a couple of hours ago than it does at midnight. And you say the Cliff Notes aren't helping? Big-time suggestion: Finish reading the book. To get there, better head to the kitchen for some sustenance and buzz—it's gonna be a long night.

[Keep Goin' Cashew, Coconut, Peanut Butter Chips, Raisin "Trail" Mix, PAGE 72]

Sometimes I just need a little bowlful of treats—quasi healthful and slightly sweet—to get me through a crammin', deadline-approaching marathon session (like finishing this book!). Here's what to make when you don't want messy, sticky, spillable foods at your desk. Or when it's time to close the books and take a hike, pack this for a snack.

2 cups salted roasted **cashews**

1 bag (10 ounces) **Reese's peanut butter chips**

2 cups (4 ounces) unsweetened **coconut chips** (See Munchie Tip)

2 cups **raisins**

It doesn't get easier than this—mix together all the ingredients and munch.

MAKES ABOUT 8 CUPS

MUNCHIE TIP
Head to the bulk-foods section of your natural-foods store for unsweetened coconut chips. These are big flakes of unsweetened dried coconut. Regular sweetened flaked coconut will do in a pinch.

All-night paper writers and test crammers know there is nothing like Red Bull for a midnight buzz. Take a brief break, whip up this great-tasting smoothie, and feel that surge straight to the brain. Now, write on!

1 cup **Häagen-Dazs raspberry sorbet**

1 cup frozen **raspberries**

1 tablespoon **honey**

1 can (8.3 ounces) **Red Bull energy drink**

Place the sorbet, raspberries, and honey in a blender. Pour the Red Bull over the top. Blend until thick and smooth. If the raspberry seeds bother you (probably not), strain the smoothie before serving. Otherwise, divide it between 2 tall glasses, or drink the whole thing yourself. Slurp and feel that energy buzz.

SERVES 2

MUNCHIE TIP
Get tropical with a Red Bull mango smoothie. Use mango sorbet instead of the raspberry. Substitute 1 cup frozen or canned cubed mango for the raspberries.

Popeye's solution for strength, power, and energy was spinach. Throw some into eggs for a protein-packed, stay-awake midnight meal.

3 large **eggs**

2 tablespoons **milk**

½ teaspoon dried **oregano**

Pinch of **salt**

Freshly ground **black pepper**

1 tablespoon **olive oil**

1 cup **baby spinach leaves**, coarsely chopped

6 **cherry tomatoes**, halved

2 tablespoons crumbled **feta cheese**

In a bowl, beat together the eggs, milk, oregano, salt, and pepper. Set aside. Place an oven rack about 4 inches from the broiler and preheat the broiler.

Heat an 8-inch sauté pan with a broilerproof handle, preferably nonstick, over medium heat. Add the oil and swirl to coat the pan. Add the spinach and sauté until wilted, about 1 minute. Add the tomatoes and sauté for 1 minute longer. Add the egg mixture. Using a spatula, scootch the eggs around in the pan until they begin to set. As you're doing this, tilt the pan and lift the edge of the omelet so some of the uncooked egg seeps underneath.

When the eggs are mostly set and lightly browned on the bottom, after about 3 minutes, sprinkle the feta over the top. Place the omelet under the broiler and cook the eggs until puffy and nicely browned, 1 to 2 minutes. Eat, think, and cram.

MAKES 1 OMELET

Women know that food feeds the soul, lifts the spirits, and gets them through those tough, high-stress times. Turn an energy bar into a warm grilled sandwich, high in calcium, full of protein, and potassium-packed with bananas. You go, girl!

1 **Luna Peanut Butter 'n Jelly bar** (See Munchie Tip)

2 slices **French bread**

$\frac{1}{2}$ **banana**, cut lengthwise into 4 thin slices

1 tablespoon **grape jelly** or strawberry jam

1 tablespoon **butter**, at room temperature

Unwrap the Luna bar and press it out flat into a 3-by-5-inch rectangle. Place it on top of one of the bread slices. Arrange the banana slices on top, and spread the jelly over the banana slices. Top with the other bread slice. Spread half the butter on the top of the sandwich.

Heat a skillet over medium heat or preheat a griddle to medium. Place the sandwich, buttered-side down, on the hot surface and grill until nicely browned, 1 to 1½ minutes. While the first side is browning, spread the remaining butter on the top of the sandwich. Flip the sandwich and brown the other side, 1 to 1½ minutes longer. Serve immediately or sooner.

MAKES 1 SANDWICH

MUNCHIE TIP
Luna bars come in so many flavors that you can invent your own grilled combos. Check out the chocolate pecan pie with bananas and skip the jelly, or try the lemon zest on cinnamon-raisin bread.

Caffeine always works for marathon work sessions, but a little sugar and cream help, too. While straight coffee eventually gives you that awful, stale-mouth taste and stomach acid buildup, this milk shake only gives you sweet calories. But, hey, you're workin' hard.

1 cup **Häagen-Dazs coffee ice cream**

1/4 cup **milk**

1/4 cup **chocolate-covered espresso beans**

Place the ice cream, milk, and espresso beans in a blender. Blend until thick and smooth.

MAKES 1 MILK SHAKE

MUNCHIE TIP
If it's going to be a long, long night and you need yet more caffeine, replace the 1/4 cup milk with 1 shot espresso and 2 tablespoons milk.

MOOD MUNCHIES

Dear Munchie Master,
I know better than to fix my mood with food, but what can I say. I snack when I'm stressed (did you know *stressed* spelled backwards is *desserts*?), I binge when I'm bummed. How do I quit this unhealthy habit?
Inner Me in Need

Dear Inner You in Need,
Quit? Did you say quit? No. Just try these healthful alternatives to lift your mood:

Eat only when you're hungry. Then eat chocolate. Exercise. Walk around the kitchen ten times before you make a snack. Eat with headphones on. Music elevates your mood and you won't hear yourself munching. Share your food with a friend. Then you can both feel guilty. Always cry into clear soups. You won't see the tears.

MM

[PMS Chocolate Fudge Fix Milk Shake, PAGE 80]

A megahit of chocolate does wonders for the PMS blues. A little buzz of caffeine doesn't hurt either. With a slight nod toward healthful munching (Oh, puh-leeze!), I've added soy milk—chocolate, of course— to this divine and mood-altering concoction. I promise, you'll slurp every last drop. Diet advice: Just throw away the ice cream container, don't even look at the calorie count.

1 pint **Ben & Jerry's Chocolate Fudge Brownie ice cream**

1/4 cup finely ground **espresso roast coffee beans**

1/2 cup **chocolate soy milk**

Place the ice cream and ground coffee beans in a blender. Pour in the soy milk. Blend until thick and smooth. Pour into 2 tall glasses, drink, grouch, and be whiny with a girlfriend.

SERVES 2

If your brain takes off in top gear when you've had eggs and toast for breakfast, then try them at midnight. Feel perky, stimulated, and protein infused with this zippy combo of scrambled eggs and pepper Jack cheese smushed—gently, of course—between the halves of a toasted bagel.

1½ teaspoons **Dijon mustard**

1½ teaspoons **mayonnaise**

2 **eggs**

1 tablespoon **milk**

Pinch of **salt**

½ cup finely shredded **pepper Jack cheese**

1 herb multigrain **bagel**

1 tablespoon **butter**

In a small bowl, mix together the mustard and mayonnaise until thoroughly blended. Set aside. In a medium bowl, beat the eggs with the milk and salt. Stir in the cheese. Cut the bagel in half and toast until golden brown. Keep warm.

Heat a small, preferably nonstick skillet over medium heat. Add the butter and swirl to coat the pan. Pour in the eggs and stir with a spatula. Nudge the eggs around in the pan until scrambled and moist. Adjust the heat so the cheese doesn't burn.

Spread the cut sides of the toasted bagel halves with the mayonnaise mixture. Top one half with the eggs. Place the other bagel half on top to form a sandwich. Eat immediately.

MAKES 1 SANDWICH

There's nothing like some crispy-hot chicken nuggets to cool down the flamed and furious. Banish the thought of ketchup and check out this spicy, lip-buzzing dipping sauce. In a flash, you'll have smoky chipotle chiles mixed into a little mayo and perked up with fresh lime—addictively good.

1 pound frozen **chicken nuggets**

½ cup **mayonnaise**

2 canned **chipotle chiles** in adobo sauce, minced, plus 1 tablespoon sauce (see Munchie Tip)

1½ teaspoons fresh **lime juice**

Preheat the oven to 400°F. Spread the chicken nuggets on a rimmed baking sheet and bake until golden brown, turning once halfway through the cooking, about 15 minutes.

Meanwhile, make the dipping sauce. In a small bowl, stir together the mayonnaise, chipotle chiles, and lime juice. Add the adobo sauce and stir to blend well.

As soon as the chicken is crispy brown, dip the nuggets in the sauce and chow down.

SERVES 2 TO 4

MUNCHIE TIP
Look for canned chipotle chiles (smoke-dried jalapeños) drenched in an adobo sauce (made from ground chiles, herbs, and vinegar) stocked with other Mexican foods in supermarkets.

Where's Mom when you need her? For those times when you are feeling blue or blah, and what you need is a bowl full of comfort but there's no chicken in sight, try this quick version of Jewish penicillin.

1 large rib **celery**, thinly sliced

2 **carrots**, peeled and thinly sliced

2 cans (14 ounces each) low-sodium **chicken broth**

1/2 cup fine **egg noodles**

Salt and freshly ground **black pepper**

Place the celery and carrots in a 2 1/2-quart saucepan. Add the chicken broth, bring to a simmer over medium heat, and cook for 5 minutes. Add the noodles and cook until tender, about 5 minutes longer. Add salt and pepper to taste.

MAKES 2 LARGE BOWLFULS

Here's a health salad that combines mood-elevating *edamame* (Japanese soybeans) with love-releasing celery. Soybeans, packed with calcium, vitamins B_1 and B_6, and phenylalanine, ought to be eaten like candy for those who want their spirits lifted. And who would have guessed that humble celery contains androsterone, a potent male hormone (think Mark McGwire) that causes the body to release an aphrodisiac scent after digestion. Whoa—better get cookin'!

4 cups **water**

1 package (1 pound) frozen ***edamame*** (soybeans in pods)

$\frac{1}{2}$ teaspoon **salt**

2 ribs **celery**

1$\frac{1}{2}$ tablespoons **mayonnaise**

1 teaspoon **white miso paste**

$\frac{1}{8}$ teaspoon Asian **sesame oil**

1 tablespoon **sesame seeds**

MUNCHIE TIP
You can buy soybeans already shelled if you don't want to bother peeling off the pods. You'll need 1$\frac{1}{4}$ cups shelled soybeans for this recipe.

In a saucepan, bring the water to a boil. Add the *edamame* and salt and simmer for 5 minutes. Drain and run under cold water until cool. Remove the beans from the pods and place them in a medium bowl. Thinly slice the celery on the diagonal, quasi-Asian style. Add to the soybeans in the bowl.

In a small bowl, mix together the mayonnaise, miso paste, and sesame oil. Stir into the soybeans and celery until thoroughly blended. Place the sesame seeds on a microwave-safe plate and microwave on high until toasty brown, about 1$\frac{1}{2}$ minutes. Alternatively, place the sesame seeds in a dry skillet and cook over medium heat, stirring constantly, until toasted, about 2 minutes.

Sprinkle the sesame seeds over the salad and serve.

SERVES 4

Breakfast at Midnight Munchies

Hypothesis:
Breakfast in the morning is unnecessary.
Coffee is all you need.

Arguments:

- If you eat late enough and eat a lot, you wake up feeling full.

- You burn fewer calories when you're sleeping; hence, there are still calories to burn when you wake up.

- It is more efficient to make breakfast at midnight because you aren't as sleepy and slow-going as in the morning.

- If you eat more and drink less late at night, you won't have to get up to pee.

Conclusion:
Breakfast at midnight.
Coffee in the morn.

[Sleepy-Making Turkey Sandwich, PAGE 90]

Become a midnight short-order cook! Turn some stale, crusty bread into the ultimo French toast. Eggy on the inside, perfumed with cinnamon and a hint of vanilla, and then blanketed with crispy flecks of cornflakes—French toast has never tasted better. Perfection is using real maple syrup.

3 large **eggs**

2 teaspoons ground **cinnamon**

½ teaspoon **salt**

1½ teaspoons **vanilla extract**

⅓ cup **milk**

4 cups **cornflakes**, finely crushed (see Munchie Tip)

½ cup or more **maple syrup**, warmed

4 to 6 slices **bread**

2 to 3 tablespoons **butter**

In a broad bowl, beat the eggs with 1½ teaspoons of the cinnamon, the salt, vanilla, and milk until thoroughly blended. Place the crushed cornflakes in a shallow pan. Add the remaining ½ teaspoon cinnamon to the maple syrup, stir to blend, and keep warm.

Preheat a large skillet over medium heat or preheat a griddle to medium. In batches (depending on how many bread slices will fit), dip each bread slice in the egg mixture, saturating both sides. Then dredge the bread in the cornflakes, coating each side well. Add a tablespoon or more of butter to the pan or griddle to coat the surface and add the bread. Cook on the first side until nicely browned, 2 to 3 minutes. Flip it and cook on the other side until browned, about 2 minutes longer. Serve immediately with the maple syrup, or keep warm in a 200°F oven while you make another batch.

SERVES 2

MUNCHIE TIP
The easiest way to crush cornflakes is to put them in a large lock-top plastic bag and pound them with a rolling pin or the bottom of a pot. However, if no one is looking and you're feeling primal, put the bag on the floor and crush them with your feet.

Everyone gets sleepy after a big Thanksgiving meal, right? The mountain-high plates of food don't help, but it's all the tryptophan in the turkey that makes those brain cells want to rest. So, if it's midnight and you can't sleep, eat turkey in your jammies!

1 **pita bread**

2 tablespoons **mayonnaise**

2 tablespoons **Ocean Spray Cran·Fruit crushed fruit** (cranberry/raspberry)

1 teaspoon prepared **horseradish**

1 cup shredded **head lettuce**

¼ pound sliced **roast turkey**

Small handful of **potato chips**

Cut the pita in half crosswise to form 2 half-moon pockets. Spread half of the mayonnaise inside each pocket. Mix together the crushed fruit and the horseradish and spread half of it inside each pita half. Stuff half of the lettuce into each pita half. Fold the turkey slices in half and layer half the slices inside each pita half. Stuff a few potato chips in each half for added crunch. Open wide, eat, and think sleepy thoughts.

MAKES 1 LARGE SANDWICH

In high school, my brother Richard was a classic breakfast-at-midnight muncher. He figured if he ate breakfast before he went to bed he wouldn't have to get up so early for class. Go figure! Here's his favorite midnight breakfast. Make sure those yolks are runny and the cheese is gooey.

1 **English muffin**, fork split

Butter, at room temperature

1 tablespoon whole-grain **Dijon mustard**

1 slice (about 1½ ounces) **Swiss cheese** (See Munchie Tip)

2 large **eggs**

Salt and freshly ground **black pepper**

Preheat the broiler. Toast the English muffin until golden brown. Smear a little butter on each half, and then spread each with the mustard. Divide the cheese between the 2 muffin halves. Place on a baking sheet and broil until melted and bubbly, about 1 minute.

Meanwhile, heat a nonstick skillet over medium heat. Add a teaspoon or so of butter and swirl to coat the pan. Crack the eggs directly into the pan—don't break the yolks! Fry on one side *only* until the whites are set and the yolks begin to set but are still runny. This will take about 2 minutes. Season with salt and pepper. Assuming the eggs have run together—they always do—cut them apart. Use a spatula to lift the eggs from the pan one at a time, and flip over directly on top of the melted cheese. Yummo—eat now.

SERVES 1

MUNCHIE TIP
Any sliced cheese will do—Cheddar, Muenster, Monterey Jack—but the bro's favorite combo is the Swiss-mustard one.

Think "blintzes drizzled with maple syrup," and you've got the flavors for these pancakes. When the breakfast mood strikes at midnight, there is nothing like a batch of hot, cheesy-rich ricotta flapjacks speckled with blueberries to satisfy the craving.

2 large **eggs**, lightly beaten

1 container (15 ounces) **ricotta cheese**

1 cup **milk**

2 tablespoons **sugar**

2 cups **Bisquick** or **Betty Crocker pancake mix** (See Munchie Tip)

1 cup fresh or frozen **blueberries** (optional)

Powdered sugar and **maple** or **berry syrup** for serving

In a large bowl, combine the eggs, ricotta, milk, and sugar. Beat until well blended. Add the pancake mix, stirring just until the flour disappears. Stir in the blueberries, if using.

Grease a pancake griddle or large skillet and preheat over medium heat. When hot, pour about ¼ cup of the batter for each pancake onto the hot surface. Cook the pancakes on the first side until they are puffed and little holes form on top, about 2 minutes. Flip and cook until nicely browned on the second side, about 2 minutes longer.

Serve on warmed plates. (See the Munchie Tip on page 95.) Dust with powdered sugar, douse with syrup, and eat 'em while they're hot.

MAKES SIXTEEN 4-INCH PANCAKES

MUNCHIE TIP
Bisquick and Betty Crocker pancake mixes call for the addition of eggs and milk. If you buy a pancake mix that requires only the addition of water, then skip adding the eggs and milk in this recipe. Mix the ricotta with 1½ cups water, blend in the sugar, and stir in the pancake mix.

Diner food at its best—sausages with pan gravy over spuds—perfect for a midnight pig out. Go for the quickie method here and use frozen hash browns and fully cooked and browned sausages. Just heat 'em and eat 'em.

2 big handfuls of frozen **hash browns** (quantities vary, this is not an exact science)

5 frozen precooked **link sausages**

2 tablespoons **butter**

½ cup **flour**

1¾ cups **milk**

½ teaspoon **salt**

Freshly ground **black pepper**

In a large skillet, panfry the hash browns according to the package directions.

While the potatoes are browning, place the sausages in a medium skillet and cook over medium heat, turning frequently, until browned and heated through, about 6 minutes.

Use the edge of a spatula to break each sausage into 4 pieces. Add the butter to the pan and stir until melted. Slowly add the flour, stirring constantly. As the flour thickens, add the milk slowly while stirring to create a smooth gravy. Add the salt and season to taste with pepper.

Divide the hash browns between 2 plates. Spoon the sausage gravy on top. Serve 'em up while they're hot.

SERVES 2 HUNGRY BUDDIES

Leftover cooked rice never tasted better. Sizzle some butter in a skillet, mix rice with a couple of beaten eggs, flatten into a pancake, and brown on both sides. Douse with warm maple syrup and catch a late-night show on the tube.

2 large **eggs**

Pinch of **salt**

1½ cups cooked **rice**

2 teaspoons **butter**

Maple syrup, warmed

In a small bowl, beat the eggs until blended and add the salt. Stir in the rice, breaking up any clumps.

In an 8-inch skillet, preferably nonstick, melt the butter over medium heat. Add the rice mixture and gently pat into a flat pancake that almost fills the pan. Cook until nicely browned on the first side, about 4 minutes. Using your best pancake-flipping skills, flip the pancake over and cook on the other side until nicely browned, about 4 minutes longer. Slip it onto a warmed plate, drench with maple syrup, and eat immediately.

MAKES ONE 7-INCH PANCAKE

MUNCHIE TIP
Picky pancake eaters like their pancakes served on warmed plates. While the rice pancake is cooking, place a plate in the sink and run very hot water over it. Leave it for a minute before drying.

Liquid Munchies

Cooling treats: A luscious liquid is welcome anytime, but at midnight it becomes a nocturnal indulgence. Break the silence of a summer night with the momentary whir of the blender, then slip outside, catch a light breeze through your nightie, and sip the divine.

Warming treats: Make in your jammies, take to bed, snuggle under the covers—this is pajama food.

Get tropical at midnight with this smooth-as-a-silk-sarong refresher. As you chill with the mango and feel the creamy coconut milk and yogurt glide across your tongue, imagine yourself slung drowsily in a hammock shaded by palms in Bali.

1½ cups diced fresh **mango**, frozen (see Munchie Tip)

1 container (6 ounces) **apricot-mango yogurt**

¾ cup unsweetened lite **coconut milk**

2 tablespoons fresh **lemon juice**

Combine the mango and yogurt in a blender. Add the coconut milk and lemon juice. Blend until smooth.

SERVES 2

MUNCHIE TIP
It isn't a big deal to dice and freeze mango, but check the freezer section of specialty-food stores like Trader Joe's or of natural-foods stores. They often stock frozen mango.

Dazzle your palate with heaps of peach flavors and a blushing hint of raspberry. This smoothie is summer in a glass—like biting into a farm-stand tree-ripened peach oozing with juice and perfumed with sweetness.

1 cup sliced frozen **peaches**, chopped

1 container (6 ounces) **peach yogurt**

1 cup peach **sorbet**

¼ cup frozen **raspberries**

Combine the peaches, yogurt, sorbet, and raspberries in a blender. Blend until smooth.

SERVES 2

This is hot chocolate for the unabashedly proud chocoholic. Falling into that club myself, I skip right past the powdery canned stuff on the shelf and go straight for the bittersweet chocolate bar. Let it melt richly and divinely in flavored cream, thin it with milk, and curl up to the best steaming mug of hot chocolate you've ever had.

1 1/2 ounces **bittersweet chocolate**, coarsely chopped

1/4 teaspoon **vanilla extract**

1/4 cup **heavy** (whipping) **cream**

2 tablespoons **sugar**

1 cup **milk**

Miniature **marshmallows** (optional)

Combine the chocolate, vanilla, cream, and sugar in a 2-cup glass measuring cup or microwave-safe bowl. Microwave on high until the cream is hot and the chocolate begins to melt, about 1 minute. Remove from the microwave and stir until smooth. Slowly pour in the milk, stirring constantly. Microwave on high until hot, 1 to 1 1/2 minutes longer. Stir to blend.

Pour into a large mug, and float marshmallows on top, if desired. Sip and be blissful.

MAKES 1 LARGE MUGFUL

MUNCHIE TIP
Easy to make stove-top version: In a small saucepan, bring the cream, vanilla, and sugar to a simmer over medium heat. Remove from the heat and stir in the chocolate until melted. Add the milk, return to the heat, and stir until hot.

Think of this as a midnight virgin margarita, blended and thick. Packed with luscious strawberries and voluptuous melon flavor, this drink gets a boost with big lime flavors. Of course, you could rim the glass with salt, and even toss in some tequila. Keep that blender whirring, invite friends, pull out the chips and salsa—party time.

2 cups cubed ripe **honeydew melon**

1 cup **lime sherbet**

2 cups frozen **strawberries**

2 tablespoons fresh **lime juice**

Pinch of **salt**

Combine the honeydew, sherbet, strawberries, lime juice, and salt in a blender. Blend until smooth.

SERVES 2

For a scratchy throat and runny nose, nothing soothes better than a hot toddy. Make this calming potion rich with spices and fragrant with the apple-like flavor of chamomile. Curl up with a steaming mugful and drift into a state of peace.

1½ cups **water**

3 quarter-size slices fresh **ginger**

1 **cinnamon stick**, 1½ inches long

¼ teaspoon ground **cloves**

1 **chamomile tea bag**

1½ tablespoons **honey**

1 to 2 tablespoons **whiskey** or **bourbon**

In a small saucepan, bring the water to a boil. Using the back of a spoon, mash the ginger to bruise it a little, which releases its flavor. Place it in a large warmed mug or small warmed teapot along with the cinnamon stick and cloves. Place the tea bag in the mug or teapot. Pour the boiling water over and allow the tea to steep for 3 to 5 minutes.

Remove the ginger and cinnamon. Gently squeeze the tea bag and remove. Stir in the honey until dissolved. Add whiskey or bourbon to taste. Drink while it's hot— relax and unwind.

SERVES 1

MUNCHIE TIP
The toddy will stay hot longer if you warm the mug teapot first. While the water is boiling, place the m or teapot in the sink and fill it with very hot water. Leave it for a minute before drying.

Fritos
CORN CHIPS
BRAND

I know
I like and ha
like an

Party Munchies

Party Munchies for Foodies and Beauties
Girls, here is pure decadence wrapped up in three fabulous recipes. Foods to munch—chips, dips, and smoothies—and home-spa fun face masks and foot soaks. Just add candles and slow-but-soulful tunes.

Beer Party Munchies
Four secrets to success: invite your buddies—the team, the dorm, the office; buy lots of brewski—ice cold; throw together some soak-up-the-suds munchables—cheap, easy, quick, with big flavors (hey, these recipes make you look like a kitchen whiz); and clean the place before your guests come—or not!

Sports Night Munchies
Here's the food to 'feed the fans: big-league finger foods; greasy, sideliner sandwiches; and chow-down chili. Nothin' fancy here—just satisfyingly good grub. Go the distance and show some class and caring with napkins and spoons and, of course, ice-*cold* beer.

[Texas-in-the-Bag Chili, PAGE 117]

Create a spa party with this cucumber dip that doubles as a face mask with the addition of coarse oatmeal! The lemon attacks the blemishes, the yogurt moisturizes the skin, and the oatmeal scrubs off those dead skin cells. Yes, indeed, girls just wanna have fun.

4 cups **plain yogurt**
(use low-fat yogurt—this is a moisturizer!)

Grated zest of 1 **lemon**

¼ cup fresh **lemon juice**

2 tablespoons chopped fresh **dill**

1 large English **cucumber**

1½ cups **mayonnaise**

1 teaspoon **salt**

½ teaspoon freshly ground **black pepper**

Crudités such as **baby carrots**, **celery sticks**, and **cauliflower** and **broccoli florets**

2 cups steel-cut or old-fashioned **rolled oats**

In a large bowl, combine the yogurt, lemon zest and juice, and the dill. Using the fine holes on a box grater, shred the cucumber (including the peel and seeds). Add to the bowl and blend thoroughly.

Pour about one third of the yogurt mixture into a serving bowl. Add the mayonnaise, salt, and pepper and blend thoroughly. Cover and chill until serving time. Serve with the crudités.

The other two thirds of the yogurt mixture becomes the facial scrub. Add the rolled oats to it, cover, and set aside until girls-glamour-and-spa-treatment time. Then, pull back your hair and wash and pat dry your face. Pat the yogurt scrub all over your face, keeping clear of the eye area. Keep the facial mask on for 10 minutes. Use a washcloth to remove the mask, always taking upward stokes to lift the skin. Splash your face with warm water and pat dry. Now, apply your favorite moisturizer.

MAKES ENOUGH DIP AND FACE MASKS FOR 4 GIRLFRIENDS

Who says chips and dips have to be appetizer fare? Brownie dough spread out on a baking sheet turns into decadently rich chocolate-chunked "chips" when cut and baked. Softened, straight-from-the-carton chocolate-cherry ice cream becomes the "dip" for this girl-party dessert fest. This is shameless indulgence.

Nonstick cooking spray for greasing pan

¼ cup **vegetable oil**

1 large **egg**

3 tablespoons **water**

1 package (15.5 ounces) **Pillsbury chocolate chunk thick 'n fudgy deluxe brownie mix**

1 to 2 pints **Ben & Jerry's Cherry Garcia ice cream**

> **MUNCHIE TIP**
> Pick any ice cream you want—mint chocolate chip, cookies-and-cream—Cherry Garcia just happens to be my favorite.

Preheat the oven to 350°F. Spray the bottom of a 10-by-15-inch rimmed baking sheet, preferably nonstick, with the cooking spray.

In a bowl, combine the oil, egg, and water and beat with a fork or wooden spoon until well blended. Stir in the brownie mix and beat until well blended. Spread evenly in the prepared pan.

Bake for 20 minutes. Remove from the oven. Use a table knife to score the brownies into about 3-inch squares. Score each square on the diagonal to form 2 triangles. Return to the oven and bake until the brownies are crisp at the edges (but not burnt), about 15 minutes longer. Place the pan on a cooling rack and let the brownies cool in the pan for 10 minutes. Use the edge of a spatula to cut the brownies at the score lines. Lift and remove the brownies from the pan and cool on a rack. They will harden and turn into "chips" as they cool.

Remove the ice cream from the freezer 20 minutes before serving. Scoop the ice cream into individual bowls and stir to make it creamy and diplike. Pass the chips and let your friends dunk and indulge.

SERVES 4 TO 6

Here is absolute indulgence and pampering for a warm summer night spa party. Gather your girlfriends, wear nightshirts, whip up this tropical splendor, and chill out and chat. Drink this divinely refreshing smoothie while soaking your feet in this sublime, foot-softening treatment. Why papaya? Not only is papaya packed with immune-boosting antioxidants and a big dose of vitamin C, but it also contains an enzyme called papain, a natural tenderizer. While you're slurping a big, nutrition-packed drink, your rough and tough feet turn into velvety tender wonders.

6 ripe **papayas**, peeled, seeded, and chopped

3 cans (20 ounces each) crushed **pineapple** in its own juice, chilled

3 cans (14 ounces each) unsweetened **coconut milk**, chilled

8 gallon-size lock-top **plastic freezer bags**

In a large bowl, using a fork or a potato masher, mash the papayas. Add the pineapple, including its juice, and mix well. Stir in the coconut milk and blend well.

To make the smoothies: Measure out 4 cups of the papaya mixture, and pour half into a blender. Blend until smooth. Pour into 2 chilled glasses. Repeat with the remaining 2 cups for the second batch.

To make the foot soak: Divide the remaining papaya mixture among the 8 plastic bags. Have your friends settle into comfortable chairs, and hand each guest her chilled smoothie, a pair of bags filled with the papaya soak, and a towel. Instruct your friends to place a foot in each bag, and suggest they mush the mixture around to coat their feet. Now, sit back and sip your smoothie, relax, and say, "Ahhhhhh." Soak for 20 to 30 minutes, rinse, and apply your favorite moisturizer.

MAKES ENOUGH SMOOTHIES AND FOOT SOAKS FOR 4 GIRLFRIENDS

Whip out a skillet, or two if you're a real kitchen jock, and toast up some of these spicy, cheesy, crispy filled tortillas. I guarantee they'll be eaten in a flash. You had better have backup supplies on hand.

10 **flour tortillas**, each 10 inches in diameter

$3/4$ pound **pepper Jack cheese**, shredded

1$2/3$ cups tomatillo **salsa** (See Munchie Tip)

Heat a large skillet over medium-high heat until hot. Place a tortilla in the pan and sprinkle with a generous $1/2$ cup of the cheese. Spoon about $1/3$ cup of the salsa over the top and spread it around. Cover with another tortilla. When the bottom tortilla is nicely browned, after about 2 minutes, use a spatula to turn the quesadilla. Cook until browned on the second side, about 2 minutes longer. Remove and keep warm while you make 4 more quesadillas with the remaining ingredients.

Use a sharp knife or pizza cutter to cut each quesadilla into 6 or 8 wedges. Arrange on a platter and serve while warm and crisp.

SERVES 8 TO 10

MUNCHIE TIP
Look for tomatillo salsa fresh in the refrigerator case or in jars on the shelf in well-stocked supermarkets. Hint: It's green.

Beer partyers love digging their hands into a bowl full of these crunchy, cheesy almonds. A smattering of mustard and a kick of cayenne make the nuts addictive. Trust me, no one will be looking for peanuts.

1 large **egg white**

1 tablespoon **Dijon mustard**

$\frac{1}{4}$ teaspoon **cayenne pepper**

1 teaspoon coarse **sea salt** or **kosher salt**

$\frac{1}{2}$ cup grated **Parmesan cheese**

3 cups (about 1 pound) raw skin-on whole **almonds**

Preheat the oven to 325°F. In a large bowl, whisk together the egg white, mustard, cayenne, and salt until well blended and smooth. Stir in the Parmesan cheese. Toss in the nuts and stir until thoroughly coated. Spread out the nuts on a rimmed baking sheet and roast for 10 minutes. Stir and then continue to roast until fragrant and nicely browned, 8 to 10 minutes longer. They'll crisp as they cool.

MAKES 3 CUPS

MUNCHIE TIP
Double the recipe if you have a crowd. These almonds freeze well. Don't bother to thaw them, just reheat at 325°F for a couple of minutes before serving.

No wimpy cheesy-topped nachos here. Big flavor rides high with spicy-hot Mexican sausage layered over your favorite chips. Douse the heat with black beans, infuse the mix with lime-and-cilantro-flavored tomatoes, and pile on the cheese. Pop the whole thing under the broiler while checkin' to make sure the six-packs are chilled.

8 cups **tortilla chips** (roughly half of a big bag)

½ pound bulk **pork chorizo**

1 can (15 ounces) **red or black beans**, drained and rinsed

1 can (10 ounces) **RO*TEL diced tomatoes** with lime juice and cilantro, drained

2 cups shredded **Cheddar cheese**

1 can (2.25 ounces) sliced ripe **olives**, drained

½ cup chopped fresh **cilantro** (optional)

Arrange the chips in a 9-by-13-inch baking pan or other large flameproof pan or dish.

Heat a medium skillet over medium-high heat. Use your hands to crumble the chorizo as you place it in the pan. Sauté the chorizo until browned and cooked through, about 5 minutes. Using a slotted spoon, remove the chorizo from the skillet and scatter it over the chips.

Sprinkle half of the black beans over the top. Spoon the diced tomatoes evenly over the beans. Top with the rest of the beans. Scatter the cheese over the entire casserole and top with the olives.

Preheat the broiler. Place the baking pan under the broiler and broil until the cheese melts and is bubbly hot, 2 to 3 minutes. Remove from the broiler and top with the cilantro, if desired. Eat the nachos while they're gooey and hot.

SERVES 4 TO 6

Score big time with a plateful of these bronzed, smoky-grilled drumettes. Throw together the marinade and let the chicken drink up those flavorings for as long as you like. A crowd of cheering friends, lots of beer, and a stack of napkins are all that's needed.

4 pounds **chicken wing drumettes** or **chicken wings**

1 bottle (16 ounces) **Jack Daniel's Sizzling Smokehouse Blend grilling sauce**

½ cup **Jack Daniel's whiskey**

½ cup Thai sweet **chile sauce** (see Munchie Tips)

½ cup dried chopped **onions**

Place the chicken in a large, heavy-duty, lock-top plastic bag. To make the marinade, combine the grilling sauce, whiskey, sweet chile sauce, and dried onions and stir well to mix. Pour over the chicken, squeeze the air out of the bag, seal the bag, and then tilt it to distribute the marinade. Set the bag in a large baking dish, just in case it leaks. Refrigerate for at least 1 hour or for up to 24 hours, turning occasionally.

Prepare a medium fire in a charcoal grill, or preheat a gas grill on medium. Remove the chicken from the marinade and space evenly apart directly over the fire. Cover the grill and cook the chicken on one side until nicely browned, about 10 minutes. Turn the pieces, cover again, and grill until the juices run clear when a piece is pierced with a knife, about 10 minutes longer. Serve immediately or keep warm until serving.

SERVES 6 TO 8

MUNCHIE TIPS

Thai sweet chile sauce is a spicy, red-pepper-flecked sauce. Look for it in the Asian foods section of well-stocked supermarkets.

If you don't feel like grilling, you can cook the drumettes in a preheated 450ºF oven. Remove the chicken pieces from the marinade and place them on 2 rimmed baking sheets. Roast for 25 minutes, switching the position of the pans halfway through the cooking time. Test for doneness by piercing with a knife; the juices should run clear. Finish under the broiler to crisp the edges and give the chicken a burnished grill look.

Guys aren't the only ones who soak up beer. Here, shrimp swim in a pool of malted barley and hops infused with garlic and a kick of red pepper flakes. Dunking them in Cajun-spice-laced mayonnaise makes them sublime. Serve with plenty of napkins. Fingers stay off the remote control when they're kept busy peeling shrimp.

1½ pounds medium **shrimp**

2 bottles (12 ounces each) **beer**, preferably a full-flavored microbrew

2 cloves **garlic**, halved

1 **bay leaf**

1 teaspoon **salt**

1 teaspoon **red pepper flakes**

Cajun Mayonnaise

1 tablespoon **Cajun seasoning blend**

1 cup **mayonnaise**

1 tablespoon fresh **lemon juice**

Rinse the shrimp, leaving the shells intact. Blot dry with paper towels. In a saucepan, combine the beer, garlic, bay leaf, salt, and red pepper flakes. Bring to a simmer, then add the shrimp. Cook the shrimp just until they turn pink, about 2 minutes. Remove from the heat and let the shrimp steep in the beer broth for 1 minute longer. Remove with a slotted spoon and set aside. Let the beer mixture cool for 20 minutes.

Return the shrimp to the beer broth, cover, and refrigerate for at least 1 hour or until ready to serve.

To make the mayonnaise: In a small bowl, mix together the Cajun seasoning and the mayonnaise. Add the lemon juice and whisk until thoroughly combined. Refrigerate until ready to serve.

When ready to serve, drain the shrimp and serve with the mayonnaise.

SERVES 8 TO 10

He-man-size sandwiches—thick, sloppy, and oozing with cheese—will stop almost any guy in his tracks. A Reuben pulled sizzlin' hot from a skillet, a beer or soda on the side, a football game on the tube, and a lazy Sunday afternoon to kill—most guys call that Paradise.

$\frac{1}{4}$ pound thinly sliced **pastrami** or **corned beef**

2 slices **rye bread**

$\frac{1}{2}$ cup **sauerkraut**

1 slice **Swiss cheese**

1 tablespoon **Thousand Island dressing**

2 tablespoons **butter**, at room temperature

Pile the pastrami on top of one slice of the bread. Drain the sauerkraut, rinse under cool water, and squeeze dry. Spread it over the pastrami, and place the cheese on top. Spread the Thousand Island dressing on the other slice of bread, and place, dressing-side down, on top of the cheese. Using half of the butter, spread it on the top piece of bread.

Heat a skillet over medium heat or preheat a griddle to medium. Place the sandwich, buttered-side down, on the hot surface and grill until nicely browned, 1 to 1$\frac{1}{2}$ minutes. While the first side is browning, spread the top piece of bread with the remaining butter. Flip the sandwich and brown the other side, about 2 minutes longer. If the cheese isn't melting, cover the pan with a lid. Serve immediately and pass the Tums later.

MAKES 1 SANDWICH

MUNCHIE TIP
Cookin' for a crowd? Make like a short-order cook and keep those towering sandwiches comin'.

China bowls are highly overrated. I mean, who needs a bowl when you can slit open a snack bag of chips, pour chili on top, and grab a spoon? They've been doing this at Texas tailgate parties for years. Nothing leaks, and there are no dishes to wash—how great is that? Fancy-up this party dish by serving bowls of sliced green onions, chopped cilantro, and sliced black olives on the side.

2 cans (15 ounces each) of your favorite **chili with beans**

2 tablespoons diced canned **jalapeño chile**

2 tablespoons **barbecue sauce**

4 bags (4 1/2 ounces each) **Fritos corn chips**

1 cup (4 ounces) shredded **Cheddar cheese**

Optional Toppings

1/2 cup chopped fresh **cilantro**

1/2 cup thinly sliced **green onions**

1/2 cup sliced **black olives**

In a small saucepan, heat the chili over medium heat until hot. Stir in the jalapeño chile and barbecue sauce.

Split open the bags of Fritos along the long back seam, and spread the bags open. Divide the cheese among the 4 bags, scattering it over the chips. Pour the chili on top, dividing it among the bags. Pass the toppings in bowls. Hand out spoons and chow down.

MAKES 4 BIG SERVINGS

The exact equivalents in the following tables have been rounded for convenience.

Liquid/Dry Measures

U.S.	METRIC
¼ teaspoon	1.25 milliliters
½ teaspoon	2.5 milliliters
1 teaspoon	5 milliliters
1 tablespoon (3 teaspoons)	15 milliliters
1 fluid ounce (2 tablespoons)	30 milliliters
¼ cup	60 milliliters
⅓ cup	80 milliliters
½ cup	120 milliliters
1 cup	240 milliliters
1 pint (2 cups)	480 milliliters
1 quart (4 cups, 32 ounces)	960 milliliters
1 gallon (4 quarts)	3.84 liters
1 ounce (by weight)	28 grams
1 pound	454 grams
2.2 pounds	1 kilogram

Length

U.S.	METRIC
⅛ inch	3 millimeters
¼ inch	6 millimeters
½ inch	12 millimeters
1 inch	2.5 centimeters

Oven Temperature

FAHRENHEIT	CELSIUS	GAS
250	120	½
275	140	1
300	150	2
325	160	3
350	180	4
375	190	5
400	200	6
425	220	7
450	230	8
475	240	9
500	260	10